SOUTHAMPTON'S CHANGING FACES

DB PUBLISHING

First published in Great Britain in 2005 by The Breedon Books Publishing Company Limited
Breedon House, 3 The Parker Centre, Derby, DE21 4SZ.

Paperback edition published in Great Britain in 2010 by The Derby Books Publishing
Company Limited, 3 The Parker Centre, Derby, DE21 4SZ.

ISBN 978-1-85983-873-0

Printed and bound by Rzeszowskie Zakłady Graficzne S.A., Poland.

ACKNOWLEDGEMENTS

I am deeply indebted to Ian Abrahams (who also kindly checked the accuracy of the location and text of the Bitterne area photos for me) and the Committee of Bitterne Local History Society for the unrestricted use of their vast photographic library (especially including their most recent additions, the *Norman Gardiner* and *Eric Thompson Collections*), also Mrs Maureen Webber for her *Henry Brain Collection* and Peter Boyd-Smith for his *Cobwebs Collection*. I am also grateful for the use of illustrations or photographs supplied by Genevieve Bailey, John Edmonds, the late Eric Gadd, Bill Moore and Dolly O'Beirne. Much of the material supplied is previously unpublished and without the assistance of the foregoing this book would not have been possible.

In addition, I am very appreciative of the help given by Mike Budd, David Harries, Chris Hunt, Tim Kenealy, Bryan Lunn, Chris Trigg, Jelle van Damme, Kevin White and Dave Wilson, all of whom provided assistance in gaining access to places where the general public are normally not allowed.

Matthew McManus BA(Hons) (with Laura Spafford BA(Hons)) and Sam Milner deserve a special mention for their very useful and meticulous help in taking a number of the modern photographs. Tribute must also be paid to the staff of the Southampton City Archives and Central Library Special Collections, whose unfailing willingness to help was, as ever, invaluable and to my editor, Susan Last, for her support and encouragement.

I must also acknowledge that much of the source material on the public houses illustrated in the book was taken from *Southampton's Inns and Taverns* by Tony Gallaher.

Finally, I must thank Joan Holt for the final proof reading and, most of all, my wife Marion for not only carrying out the initial proof read but also tolerating my prolonged absences during the book's compilation.

J.W.M. Brown

FOREWORD

Building developments, some dramatic, have transformed sections of the city over the years. The Victorian buildings, with their ornate grandeur, were designed to impress and display the owner's wealth and social standing, whether as a private individual or in business. On the other side of the coin, Victorian slums were a blot on the town and many pressed for drastic improvements. Changing social attitudes and consequent 'modernisation' following World War One resulted in the reconstruction of many such buildings.

Southampton also suffered severe and widespread damage during World War Two, and the post-war restoration altered many large areas beyond recognition. Further changes came in the 1950s when a new ring road was constructed around the city centre to cope with ever-increasing traffic demands and again in the 1970s when the massive Itchen Bridge was built to provide an improved connection with the eastern area of the city. The Bitterne suburb was also transformed in the 1980s when a new bypass tore through the former village.

Fortunately, some individuals had the foresight to take photographs before properties were demolished, and this has given me access to invaluable and often unpublished material. Among them are:

Bitterne Local History Society (www.bitterne.net), formed in 1981 when the new bypass was proposed and now with well over 200 members. They have amassed a collection of nearly 3,000 photographs as well as many irreplaceable artefacts, housed in their Heritage & Research Centre at 225 Peartree Avenue near the heart of the old village.

Norman Gardiner (1901–1988), a former Legal Executive with local solicitors Bell, Pope and Bridgewater in their Woolston office. An enthusiastic photographer in his early years, he developed a deep interest in researching local history following his retirement, collecting many local postcard scenes. He constantly endeavoured to rekindle people's memories of the lost areas of Southampton.

Eric Thompson (1931–1999), an enthusiastic member of Bitterne Local History Society who ran his own plumbing business and never travelled without his camera. He took many photographs on behalf of the Society, as well as videoing events, and had a passion for capturing local scenes before developers moved in. He was also an avid postcard collector of local views. Both Norman and Eric generously contributed photographs to the Veal Collection, held by the Southampton City Archives, as well as to Bitterne Local History Society.

Henry Brain (1873–1952), who was a builder with a hobby of photographing local scenes and producing postcards as a secondary form of income. His personal albums of photographs taken during the period 1890–1910 survived a parachute mine attack during World War Two, and his grandaughter, Mrs Maureen Webber, allowed me full access to them. They formed the basis of my book *Henry Brain, a Victorian and Edwardian Photographer*, available from Bitterne Local History Society, Southampton.

Peter and Jan Boyd-Smith are well known in Southampton as the owners of Cobwebs, an award-winning shop specialising in memorabilia from ocean liners. Established in 1975, they have supplied items, both large and small, to collectors, museums and film and television companies worldwide. They are the authors of a number of publications on maritime subjects as well as local history books, including *Southampton – Gateway to England* and *Southampton in Focus*, and have amassed a large collection of local photographs and postcards.

I am indebted to all of the above.

Research while compiling this book has highlighted the many friendly corner shops falling victim to competition from giant superstores and being replaced by housing. The remorseless march of sometimes rapacious developers is also well nigh unstoppable. I have, therefore, attempted to take the reader through a nostalgic tour of old Southampton with selected pictures from the above collections and their modern counterparts taken from, as far as physically possible, the same position. I hope they arouse happy memories.

Lower High Street *c.*1885. The Vine Hotel on the left, just past the entrance of Porter's Lane, and the Sun Hotel on the right corner both date back to 1783. The Holy Rood Church spire in the distance is on the corner of Bridge Street. *(Eric Gadd)*

The Luftwaffe completely destroyed this end of the High Street in World War Two, but exposed mediaeval vaults still remain on the left. The former Sun Hotel has been replaced by a pleasant office block. *(Sam Milner)*

Centre High Street *c.*1828, looking north, with the balcony of the Audit House on the left and the spire of Holy Rood Church clearly visible. The *c.*1760 St Lawrence Church in the middle distance does not yet have its distinctive spire. *(Jim Brown)*

Another view, *c.*1895, but from just beyond the junction with Bridge Road (renamed Bernard Street in 1924) and, therefore, only showing part of Holy Rood Church. The St Lawrence Church spire is now clearly visible. *(Jim Brown)*

The flag on the right is advertising the Continental Café and Restaurant, and St Lawrence Church spire is in the centre, photographed *c.*1905. The electric tramcar service started in 1900, initially on the Shirley/The Junction route. *(Cobwebs Collection – Peter Boyd-Smith)*

St Lawrence Church was demolished in 1925 as redundant, and Holy Rood Church was almost destroyed in the World War Two bombing raids. Minus its spire, it is now the town's Merchant Navy Memorial. *(Sam Milner)*

Upper High Street, *c*.1897, looking north, with the pillars of All Saints Church, built in 1792, on the corner of East Street. The horse-drawn tram had to travel through the centre of the Bargate and compete with the hansom cabs. *(Henry Brain Collection – Maureen Webber)*

The clock of Michael Emanuel, watchmaker & jeweller, is at No.11 High Street, on the corner of East Street. The gentleman on the left, with the dog and tall top hat, is clearly staring at the photographer, taken *c*.1900. *(Cobwebs Collection – Peter Boyd-Smith)*

The dome-roofed trams were specially designed in 1923 to pass through the Bargate arches, and Emanuel, jeweller & watchmaker, is still on the corner of East Street next to the Westminster Bank in this photograph taken *c.*1930. *(Eric Thompson Collection – Bitterne Local History Society)*

The tramcars were replaced by buses in 1950, and Emanuel's has been demolished. However, the Westminster Bank, now Natwest Bank, still exists but directly on the corner of the widened East Street. *(Sam Milner)*

This early water colour of Upper High Street, *c*.1812, looking south from the top of the Bargate, shows why in the mid-18th century it was said of the High Street 'for breadth, length and cleanliness it can scarcely be equalled in England'. *(Eric Gadd)*

This painting, *c*.1828, from further down, gives a closer view of the impressive All Saints Church at the top of East Street and shows an increased and uncontrolled mix of traffic and pedestrians on the cobbled road. *(Jim Brown)*

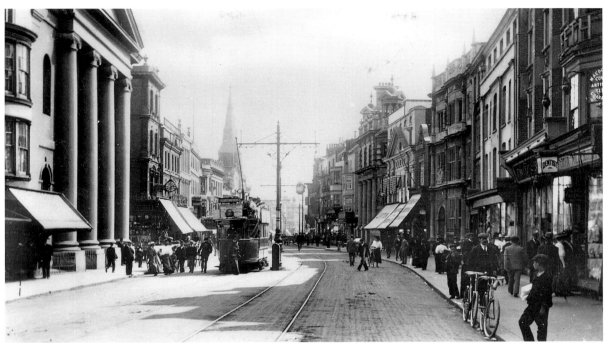

The newly electrified tram car is passing All Saints Church at the top of East Street having travelled from the Town Quay, and the imposing spire of St Lawrence Church can just be seen in the background, photographed *c.1908*. *(John Edmonds)*

The last tram ran in 1950 and was replaced by buses. The massive bombing in this area destroyed All Saints Church and almost all of the former shops. This end of the High Street is now partially pedestrianised. *(Sam Milner)*

The Gaiety opened in September 1914 on the site of Lipton's Grocers, and in 1929 it showed Southampton's first 'talkie', Al Jolson's *The Singing Fool*. This photograph of High Street was taken just prior to it closing in April 1956. *(Eric Thompson Collection – Bitterne Local History Society)*

The former pleasant looking cinema and adjacent Misselbrook & Weston's store have been replaced by nondescript offices, the Solent Blue Line ticket office and Barclay's Bank, all of little architectural merit. *(Jim Brown)*

Looking down an empty East Street, *c*.1950, from the High Street end. On the left, just beyond the bombed and overgrown ruins of All Saints Church, is Montague Burton Ltd, tailors, at No.4 in front of York Buildings. *(Eric Thompson Collection – Bitterne Local History Society)*

East Street is now one-way with congested, metered car parking. The shops were rebuilt in 1956, and the entrance of York Buildings, further down on the left, now gives access to the Bargate Shopping Centre. *(Jim Brown)*

Lower East Street *c.*1950. This shows the utter devastation caused by wartime bombing with the ruins of the former Edwin Jones Department Store and shops on both sides. The then Methodist Central Hall can just be seen at the far end. *(Eric Thompson Collection – Bitterne Local History Society)*

Now called Debenhams, the store was rebuilt in 1957, and modern shops have replaced the bombed ruins. The East Street Shopping Centre at the bottom blocks the view of the now Community Church Central Hall. *(Jim Brown)*

Sometimes mistakenly called the East Gate, this access through the north wall of the old town was called York Gate and was constructed in 1769 to give a new entrance to Hanover and York Buildings from nearby East Street, photographed *c.*1900. *(Cobwebs Collection – Peter Boyd-Smith)*

York Gate, which now provides access to the Bargate Shopping Centre, became unsafe and was demolished in 1961. Vincent's Walk and the parks adjoining Hanover Buildings can just be seen in the distance. *(Sam Milner)*

Upper High Street, *c.*1895, looking up at the south face of the Bargate with the statue of George III in Roman costume in the centre niche. The absence of overhead cables shows that the tramcars are still horse drawn. *(Eric Gadd)*

The tramcars are now electrified, and Henry Chard, the gentlemen's outfitter, proudly boasts of having been established for 60 years. The adjacent large insurance block will soon be demolished for traffic access, photographed *c.*1930. *(Cobwebs Collection – Peter Boyd-Smith)*

The small left-hand archway provides a pedestrian access through the Bargate, photographed *c.*1933. This eastern circuit was opened up in 1932, and the circuit right around the Bargate was completed on the western side in June 1938. *(Cobwebs Collection – Peter Boyd-Smith)*

The eastern circuit has now been pedestrianised, and the electric tram cars have been replaced by buses. On the centre right, just out of sight, is the entrance to the Bargate Shopping Arcade that leads directly to East Street. *(Sam Milner)*

The original lions guarding the ancient Bargate were made of wood and needed to be varnished, in 1619. The present lions are made of lead and were cast in 1743. Behind them is Pembroke Square, now replaced by modern shops. *(Genevieve Bailey)*

Looking west, as opposed to the east above, Bargate Street originally led directly to the Western Shore and was lined with small shops and housing. Still with shops, it now leads to the West Quay shopping complex. *(Sam Milner)*

Bargate Street in 1960. This led to Western Esplanade and Pirelli's cable factory. Work has just started on opening up Portland Terrace as a new ring road, and the Old Arundel Tower Hotel, opened *c.1853*, will soon be demolished. *(Eric Thompson Collection – Bitterne Local History Society).*

More dramatic changes came about in 1998 when the massive West Quay development took place just west of the enlarged 1960s ring road. A new pedestrian tunnel (on the right) now gives access to the lower area. *(Jim Brown)*

The Bargate *c.*1760. This view of the north face was made before the eastern archway was constructed in 1764. Either side of the archway are large paintings, both now in the museum, of the legendary Sir Bevis and his giant Ascupart. *(Norman Gardiner Collection – Bitterne Local History Society)*

Ever-increasing shops are encroaching on the ancient Bargate, *c.*1895, and the Scrase's Star Brewery's Coachmaker's Arms, demolished in 1904 to make room for a new police station, is adjoining on the right. *(Cobwebs Collection – Peter Boyd-Smith)*

SHOP AT BARGATE!

Enquiries
for
Shops and Offices

EAST BARGATE DEVELOPMENT CO.
2 Bargate, Southampton
Telephone : 3406

OR MAIN AGENTS:
HECTOR YOUNG, F.A.I.
Southampton. Telephone: 2646

The former Pembroke Square, *c.*1935, on the east of the Bargate, has now been completely demolished and replaced by a new parade of shops. The cupola of All Saints Church can be seen in the centre background. *(Cobwebs Collection – Peter Boyd-Smith)*

The area is now partially pedestrianised, and the modern Bargate Centre leads right through to East Street. There are current plans to extend the pedestrianised area to link up with the adjacent shopping precinct. *(Sam Milner)*

Above Bar, *c*.1904, looking south, with Sussex Place terrace on the left. The Royal Southampton Yacht Club is on the right, on the corner of Manchester Street, followed by Ogle Road and the Church of Christ in the background. *(Cobwebs Collection – Peter Boyd-Smith)*

Sussex Place has been replaced by shops, and the entrance to the Marlands Shopping Centre now covers the mouth of the vanished Manchester Street. The Above Bar Church is now on the upper floor of its old site. *(Sam Milner)*

This time looking north, *c.*1908, with the Royal York Palace of Varieties on the immediate left. Bought in 1926 by the then adjacent *Southern Echo* newspaper to enlarge their premises, it was destroyed in the blitz of 1940. *(John Edmonds)*

The rebuilt *Southern Daily Echo* transferred its operation to Redbridge in 1996, following that the building was demolished and replaced by this striking entrance to the massive West Quay Shopping Centre. *(Jim Brown)*

Above Bar *c*.1948. The popular Sussex Hotel was on the corner of Sussex Terrace, leading directly to Palmerston Park, and next to the Freeman, Hardy & Willis shoe store, Halford's cycle company and Parkhouse & Wyatt jewellers. *(Eric Thompson Collection – Bitterne Local History Society)*

Although the Sussex Hotel survived the wartime blitz, it succumbed to post-war developers and closed in 1967. Only Parkhouse & Wyatt remains in-situ, the other stores having changed owners several times. *(Sam Milner)*

Opened as the Regal Cinema in 1934 and changed to the Odeon in 1945 (photographed *c.*1975), this well-frequented, popular cinema was built on the site of the 1865 Philharmonic Hall that became the Alexandra Theatre in 1910. *(Eric Thompson Collection – Bitterne Local History Society)*

The Odeon closed its doors in September 1993 and was demolished, together with the adjacent Portland Arms that was frequented by local newspaper reporters. These pleasant modern stores were built on the site. *(Jim Brown)*

Above Bar *c.*1936. This stretch was dominated by two cinemas, the Classic, next door to Parkhouse & Son, ('Wyatt' was included in 1940) and the Picture House. The latter opened in 1920, although with only a small front, seating 1,600. *(Eric Thompson Collection – Bitterne Local History Society)*

This area suffered in the blitz of November 1940 when the Picture House was completely destroyed and the Classic, opened in 1937, was severely damaged but survived until it closed in January 1978. *(Sam Milner)*

Looking south, *c.*1895, with the offices of the London & South West Railway Company on the right. This building was once the Clock Tower Cinema, seating 500, from 1920 to 1923 and became Lloyds Bank in 1925. *(Norman Gardiner Collection – Bitterne Local History Society)*

During the building of the Civic Centre in the early 1930s, a section of Above Bar, including nearby Thorner's Charity, was bought by the Council to construct the above Civic Centre Road access to the west. *(Matt McManus)*

Above Bar, *c.*1900, looking west from the top of New Road, with the side entrance to the Grand Theatre on the right. The 1889 Clock Tower was a bequest of Mrs Henrietta Sayers to supply drinking water for dogs, horses and people. *(Henry Brain Collection – Maureen Webber)*

The Grand Theatre has been replaced by the large Marlands office block, and the former Above Bar buildings were destroyed in World War Two. The clock tower was moved to Bitterne Park Triangle in 1934. *(Sam Milner)*

Looking north along Above Bar, *c*.1905, one can see Moira House just behind the Clock Tower. It was named after the Earl of Moira, whose army to assist French Royalists was temporarily based in the town in 1794–5. (*John Edmonds*)

New Road is wider and Moira House was completely rebuilt in 1964. It is currently New Oxford House, the home of the Nationwide Building Society, and vehicle access along these roads is now much more restricted. (*Sam Milner*)

Upper Above Bar Street, *c.*1906, looking north towards The Junction, with part of Thorner's Charity Almshouse on the left, in front of the tiny Gibbs Road. The adjacent terraced properties housed many dentists and surgeons along its length. *(Norman Gardiner Collection – Bitterne Local History Society)*

The top end of Above Bar Street, *c.*1930, with Plummer Roddis department store, opened in 1896, displaying its wares next to the Birmingham & Coventry Motor & Cycle shop at No.185. Prospect Place is on the right. *(John Edmonds)*

These temporary shops headed by C&A Modes and with Plummer Roddis department store at the far end, photographed *c.*1946, were erected after the upper length of Above Bar Street was completely destroyed in the 1940 blitz. *(Eric Thompson Collection – Bitterne Local History Society)*

Guildhall Square was left open when the final post-war rebuilding took place, and the new Plummer Roddis store was taken over by the Southampton Institute. This was established in 1984 and has now been granted the title of Southampton Solent University. *(Sam Milner)*

The Junction, *c.*1890, looking south with what was then Tyrrell & Green's drapery store on the corner of Commercial Road. The horse-drawn tram has just passed Prospect Place en route to Portswood via London Road. *(Eric Thompson Collection – Bitterne Local History Society)*

Photographed *c.*1908, Tyrrell's has now changed from Plummer, Roddis and Tyrrell to just Plummer Roddis, and the open-top tram is now electrified. The town's first electric tram travelled from The Junction to Shirley in 1900. *(Cobwebs Collection – Peter Boyd-Smith)*

The Tudor Buildings on the left, *c.*1950, next to Prospect Place, with the familiar names of the Tudor Restaurant, Eric's, Murdoch, Austin Reed, Swears & Wells, Elam, John Farmer, and the Southern Gas Board showrooms. *(Norman Gardiner Collection – Bitterne Local History Society)*

The Gas Board showrooms have been transformed into the large Old Fat Cat public house, and the former Prospect Place shops became Tyrrell & Green's store, which are now empty and awaiting further development. *(Matt McManus)*

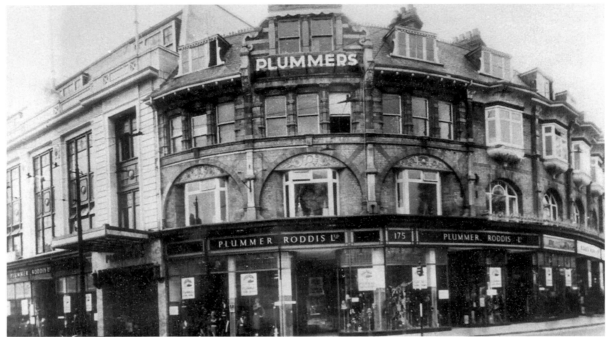

The Junction *c.*1935. William Plummer started his drapery business in Eastbourne in 1873 and soon expanded into other towns. This fine Southampton store opened in 1896 and sold a wide range of clothing and household furnishings. *(Eric Thompson Collection – Bitterne Local History Society)*

Destroyed in the 1940 blitz and rebuilt in 1963, it is now the Southampton Solent University Conference Centre. In 1994 it was renamed the Sir James Matthews Building after a popular local politician and educationalist. *(Jim Brown)*

The Junction in 1897. An unfamiliar view to most Sotonians, this was a mock gateway erected in front of The Junction to celebrate Queen Victoria's Diamond Jubilee. Andrews Park is on the left and West Marlands on the right. *(Henry Brain Collection – Maureen Webber)*

An unusual traffic-free view in the town with its traffic restriction on vehicles entering from the London Road junction. The Cenotaph is just out of sight on the right in what is now Watts Park. *(Matt McManus)*

Brunswick Place *c.*1904. St Andrew's Presbyterian Church, built in 1853 on the corner of Brunswick Place and Dorset Street, was known as the 'Scotch Church'. The site was donated by Andrew Lamb, a senior engineer of the P&O Line. *(Cobwebs Collection – Peter Boyd-Smith)*

St Andrew's Church became redundant. It was demolished in 1995 and replaced by the modern Brunswick Gate office block. Opposite is the Charlotte Place 270-bedroom Jurys Inn under construction. *(Jim Brown)*

East Park Terrace *c.*1895. This was a desirable area next to Andrew's Park, and, as a boy, Viscount Jellicoe lived at No. 26 in the 1860s. The corner block at the top of St Andrew's Road later became the Walpole Dispensary. *(Norman Gardiner Collection – Bitterne Local History Society)*

The terrace was demolished in 1960 to make way for an office block, new ambulance station and the Southampton Institute of Higher Education It now includes the more recent Mountbatten Library. *(Matt McManus)*

St Mary's Road *c*.1910. The Territorial Army Drill Hall was erected in 1889 and was used by several volunteer units. The adjacent premises of G. Rice at No. 118 has a plaque marked 'Queensland Steam Bakery 1895' above the window. *(Dolly O'Beirne)*

The Drill Hall is now the St Mary's Leisure Centre, and George Rice's bakery has been replaced by the Southampton Community Drug Agency. The road on the left leads to the large Charlotte Place roundabout. *(Jim Brown)*

London Road *c*.1916. This shows Southampton's first purpose-built public library at the junction with Cumberland Place. It was opened in 1893 at a cost of £4,500. Destroyed in the bombing of 1940, it was an empty site for many years. *(Norman Gardiner Collection)*

The well designed, large office block of Paris, Smith and Randell Solicitors has replaced the library and has the address of No. 1 London Road. Traffic lights are now plentiful throughout the city! *(Jim Brown)*

St Paul's Church, built in 1828, is prominent in this view of London Road, looking north *c.*1920. Opposite the church one can just see the canopy of the Carlton Cinema, 45 London Road, opened in 1914 but closed by 1923. *(Norman Gardiner Collection – Bitterne Local History Society)*

Almost all of the buildings shown in the earlier view were destroyed in World War Two and the post-war reconstruction was completed by the mid-1960s. Traffic is now much more of a problem. *(Jim Brown)*

London Road *c*.1939. The Unitarian Church stands on the corner of Bellevue Road next to Benjamin Warden's home and greengrocery shop at No. 62. The National Provincial Bank is on the left on the corner of Carlton Crescent. *(Norman Gardiner Collection – Bitterne Local History Society)*

The Unitarian Church and the adjacent grocery shop were destroyed in the 1940 bombing, and estate agents Sawbridge & Sons and Fox & Sons are now advertising Benjamin Warden's vacant plot for sale, *c*.1946. *(Eric Thompson Collection – Bitterne Local History Society)*

Much of London Road was destroyed in the blitz of 1940, as shown in this view looking south. The badly damaged Lloyds Bank, on the right, somehow managed to continue business until it later relocated, photograped *c*.1950. *(Eric Thompson Collection – Bitterne Local History Society)*

Moore and Blatch Solicitors have a large office block on the site of the Unitarian Church, and The Varsity public house has replaced Lloyds Bank, but otherwise the post-war development has little architectural merit. *(Matt McManus)*

Bedford Place, *c.*1938, looking north from Cumberland Place with the access road on the left leading to the popular coach station in Grosvenor Square. On the right at Waterloo Terrace is the newly erected Ye Red Lion public house. *(Eric Thompson Collection – Bitterne Local History Society)*

The coach station was demolished and not reinstated, and the former booking office is now an office block. The now just Red Lion was temporarily called the Tut and Shive, the meaning of which escapes the author! *(Matt McManus)*

Windsor Terrace *c.*1905. The Grand Theatre opened on 28 November 1898 as the New Hippodrome and was frequented by such performers as Sarah Bernhardt, Henry Irving and Lillie Langtry. It closed in October 1959. *(Henry Brain Collection – Maureen Webber)*

Local government staff now occupy the multi-storey Marlands House office block, built in 1962 on the site of the Grand Theatre, with ground-floor shops and offices facing what is now Civic Centre Road. *(Jim Brown)*

Windsor Terrace *c.*1950. The side of the Grand Theatre is on the left next to Plested's Pie Shop (now relocated to East Street) where waiting queues for the theatre could see through the large window and smell the delicious pies being made. *(Eric Thompson Collection – Bitterne Local History Society)*

Marlands House replaced the theatre and pie shop, and the shops shown in 1950 were demolished. In 1960 their replacements were also demolished when the Marlands Shopping Centre was built in 1989. *(Jim Brown)*

Looking along Windsor Terrace towards the Civic Centre, *c.*1947, with a now derelict site on the right and the Grand Theatre at the rear. The extremely useful Hants & Dorset Bus Station on the left was not replaced. *(Eric Thompson Collection – Bitterne Local History Society)*

Windsor Terrace is now merely a secure service area for the Marlands Shopping Centre, which has replaced the bus station and upper Above Bar shops. The large Marlands House office block dominates the area. *(Jim Brown)*

Windsor Terrace in 1988. A view from the top of Marlands House at the start of the construction of the Marlands Shopping Centre. Part of Manchester Street's terrace, seen right in the foreground, is still preserved inside the Shopping Centre. *(Jim Brown)*

The Marlands Shopping Centre was completed in 1991 on the site of the former Hants & Dorset Bus Station. The twin Arundel Tower blocks, seen here in 1988, were demolished in 1998 for the West Quay Centre. *(Jim Brown)*

Civic Centre Road in 1932. The Duke and Duchess of York, later King George VI and Queen Elizabeth, inaugurating the new road in front of the Civic Centre on 6 July 1932. The clock tower was not completed until 1933. *(Norman Gardiner Collection - Bitterne Local History Society)*

The completed clock tower chimes out *Oh God Our Help in Ages Past* every four hours, from 8am to 8pm, and the former Thorner's Charity Home on the right corner (its wall visible in the 1932 photograph) has been replaced by a block of shops. *(Jim Brown)*

Civic Centre Road *c.*1960. The Grand Theatre and the Hants & Dorset bus station were well-known features in the town centre, as was the attractive fountain with its multi-coloured lights and wonderful display of roses. *(Cobwebs Collection – Peter Boyd-Smith)*

The bus station and adjacent Lord Louis public house were replaced by the Marlands Shopping Centre in 1998. The fountain was also later removed to allow for major road improvements to the main west route. *(Jim Brown)*

On 6 November 1940 several 500lb bombs dropped on the Civic Centre, including the front of the Art Gallery above and the nearby School of Art, where 14 children from Central School were killed. *(Cobwebs Collection – Peter Boyd-Smith)*

A new and impressive façade and entrance now gives access to the city's internationally-known Art Gallery, and the fountain has been relocated from Civic Centre Road to the building's north-facing forecourt. *(Jim Brown)*

Civic Centre Road in 1938. The vast Power Station, built *c.*1903, dominates the view looking west towards Millbrook. It was demolished in 1977 when commercial development started on the 1930s reclaimed New Docks area. *(Eric Thompson Collection – Bitterne Local History Society)*

Toys R Us is now on the site of the former Power Station, and large blocks of student accommodation have replaced the former houses along Civic Centre Road. Central Railway Station also has a new look. *(Jim Brown)*

Civic Centre Road *c*.1938. This not only shows the vast size of the generating station but also the new façade of Southern Railway's West Station, renamed Central Station in 1935. Rail parcels were collected from the office in the foreground. *(Eric Thompson Collection – Bitterne Local History Society)*

Heavy foliage now obstructs the view from the previous 1938 photograph's position. The tall power station chimneys have long gone and were replaced by Toys R Us (not visible). What is prominent, however, is the massive Skandia Insurance block. *(Jim Brown)*

This 1973 view of Havelock Road shows the front of the Law Courts with the Marlands Hall, then housing the Juvenile Court, directly opposite. The Hants & Dorset bus station is just behind and left of the Civic Centre clock tower. *(Eric Thompson Collection – Bitterne Local History Society)*

Marlands Hall has been replaced by the BBC Broadcasting House, and the large Marlands Shopping Centre now occupies the site of the former bus station. It is dwarfed by the massive Skandia Life Insurance block. *(Jim Brown)*

Commercial Road, *c.*1970, showing the Refuge Assurance Company, cafés and the Gaumont Theatre, opened as The Empire in 1928 but changed to Gaumont in 1950 when it showed live performances as well as films. *(Bitterne Local History Society)*

The offices and buildings have been swept away to prepare for large-scale development at the junction with Havelock Road. The theatre changed its name to the Mayflower in 1987 and is renowned for its West End shows. *(Jim Brown)*

Polygon Hotel *c.*1960. This popular local hotel was built in 1937 on the site of the 18th-century Polygon House, so called because the original concept was a circle of 12 large houses with long gardens tapering like the spokes of a wheel. *(Bill Moore)*

This large block of 60 flats replaced the hotel in 2002 and bears a plaque explaining that the 14th Major Port, US Army, responsible for planning D Day troop movements were quartered here in World War Two. *(Matt McManus)*

Burton Road *c.*1974. The late Victorian houses of this cul-de-sac are viewed from Milton Road looking towards Archers Road, with St Mark's Church of England School on the distant far left and its church on the right. *(Eric Thompson Collection – Bitterne Local History Society)*

The church and buildings connected with St Marks Church of England School were demolished in 1983, but a modern St Mark's Church and Hall were rebuilt on the same site. The school transferred to Western Secondary School in 1968. *(Jim Brown)*

Milton Road *c.*1976. The Southampton 'Saints' football club, their home then at the St Mary's Antelope ground, played their first match in 1885. They moved to The Dell in 1898 and this shows the exterior of the Milton Road Stand. *(Eric Thompson Collection – Bitterne Local History Society)*

The 'Saints' have now moved to new imposing premises near their original home in St Mary's, and their former site was developed into a massive housing complex, with the Crossley Place section seen on the left. *(Jim Brown)*

Burlington Road *c.*1952. The shop was the premises of G. Scriven, grocer, greengrocer, confectioner and provisioner, at Nos.1 and 3 on the corner with Sandhurst Road, one of many useful small shops that served the neighbourhood. *(Eric Thompson Collection – Bitterne Local History Society)*

A story that is repeated throughout the city and this book: competition from the large, multinational stores, especially the large out-of-town, drive-in ones, makes the small, neighbourhood shop unprofitable. *(Jim Brown)*

Millbrook Road *c.*1960. Paynes Road sweeps up to the left towards Shirley Road, and the busy Millbrook Road connects the town with the west. Ted Haresign and his wife managed the popular filling station at the junction for many years. *(Eric Thompson Collection – Bitterne Local History Society)*

Paynes Road continues to Shirley Road, but Millbrook Road is now the wide A33 dual carriageway and underpass that leads into the town centre and the docks via Mountbatten Way and West Quay Road. *(Jim Brown)*

A view from the top of the then Post House Hotel, *c.*1973, with the Civic Centre clock tower in the centre and the vast complex of the Pirelli General Cable Works in the foreground. The power station is at the extreme left. *(Eric Thompson Collection – Bitterne Local History Society)*

The Civic Centre is now obscured by the Skandia Asssurance building, Pirelli General replaced by the West Quay development and the power station and Arundel Tower twin office blocks have been demolished. *(Jim Brown)*

Western Esplanade *c.*1900. The town swimming baths opposite Manchester Street were constructed in 1891 and the left side of the building, with Turkish Baths, was for males only, with the female baths on the far right. No mixed bathing! *(Cobwebs Collection – Peter Boyd-Smith)*

The baths have been replaced by the massive multi-storey car park that serves the adjacent modern Asda Superstore and the Marlands Centre, which has incorporated part of Manchester Street within its complex. *(Jim Brown)*

Maddison Street *c.1952*. The small groceries and provisions shop of Mrs E.D. Maggs on the corner also served adjacent Castle Square, where the novelist Jane Austen had lived with her family from 1806 to 1809. *(Eric Thompson Collection – Bitterne Local History Society)*

Developers had replaced the Victorian terrace with modern accommodation by 1985, but the outer wall of Southampton Castle was left untouched. Maddison Street was first mentioned in local directories in 1880. *(Jim Brown)*

Portland Terrace *c.*1960. The south, cul-de-sac end of the road with the Royal Victoria Assembly Rooms opened in 1820 as the centre of the town's social life. Later occupied by the Gas Company, it was demolished in 1961 for the ring road. *(Eric Thompson Collection – Bitterne Local History Society)*

The adjacent Coliseum opened in 1910 to replace a skating rink on the site, photographed *c.*1960. The largest meeting hall and interior sports venue in Southampton, it was later used as a postal sorting office. *(Eric Thompson Collection – Bitterne Local History Society)*

The lower end of Portland Terrace, no longer a cul-de-sac, and the large Arundel Towers office blocks on the right, built in 1968 and photographed *c.*1973. Extended *Daily Echo* offices have replaced the former Coliseum building. *(Eric Thompson Collection – Bitterne Local History Society)*

The massive West Quay Shopping Centre construction meant removing the twin tower blocks in 1997 to provide an entrance bridging a lowered Portland Terrace. The *Echo* offices have relocated to Redbridge. *(Jim Brown)*

Portland Terrace, *c*.1959, looking north, with Manchester Street bisecting the road just beyond the parked cars. Everton Street, in the far distance, leads up to the Civic Centre. These private houses were built in the late 1850s. *(Eric Thompson Collection – Bitterne Local History Society)*

The construction of the Inner Ring Road in 1960, that replaced the former Portland Terrace, and the multi-storey car park, taking the place of the houses in the 1970s, have made dramatic changes to the area. *(Jim Brown)*

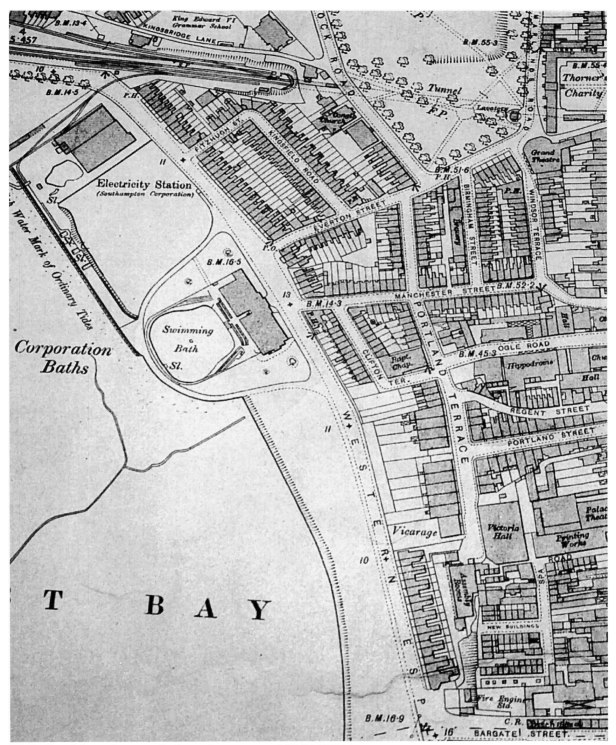

Reproduced from the 1910 Ordnace Survey map. NC/03/17894
This 1910 map will revive memories of the Power Station and Baths in Western Esplanade, the cul-de-sac
Portland Terrace and the West Marlands pleasure ground before the construction of the Civic Centre.

Portland Terrace, *c.*1973, photographed from the top of the now demolished Arundel Towers office block, showing part of the former bus station on the right and a large car park and open space to the left of the Civic Centre. *(Eric Thompson Collection – Bitterne Local History Society)*

This closest possible comparison was taken from the top of the West Quay Shopping Centre. It shows how the Marlands Centre and Skandia Life Insurance building have replaced the bus station and car parking area. *(Jim Brown)*

Photographed from the same position as before, *c.*1973, this view is further to the west, clearly showing the large chimneys of the power station and the extremely popular Lido, the town's outside swimming baths. *(Eric Thompson Collection – Bitterne Local History Society)*

The 1973 view is now much blocked but is sufficient to show that Toys R Us has replaced part of the power station. The western end of the former open-air Lido site lies between the two right-hand roundabouts. *(Jim Brown)*

Portland Terrace in 1998. The Arundel Towers blocks have been demolished, and Portland Terrace now looks like a bomb site! A new and massive John Lewis store is under construction in the left background with Portland Street to its right. (*Jim Brown*)

The bridge over Portland Terrace connects with the High Street pedestrian precinct and blocks the earlier view along Portland Terrace. The entrance to the West Quay Centre houses a large Waterstones book store. (*Jim Brown*)

Western Esplanade in 1998. The former sprawling Pirelli General site is now only a distant memory, and Western Esplanade cannot be seen, but the River Test is visible in the background. The temporary huts on the left house an army of workmen. *(Jim Brown)*

Now completed, the large Marks & Spencer store dominates the adjoining waste ground that awaits further development. The multi-storey car parks at the rear can comfortably hold over 4,000 cars. *(Jim Brown)*

Arundel Tower, photographed *c.*1900, was a drum tower, 22ft in diameter and 60ft high, guarding the north-west corner of the old mediaeval town. The Old Tower Inn, seen here at the bottom of Bargate Street, was rebuilt in 1899. *(Henry Brain Collection – Maureen Webber)*

The public house and the bottom section of Western Esplanade were swept away when the West Quay shopping development took place in 1998, but access is still possible to Bargate Street via steps. *(Jim Brown)*

Albion Place, *c.*1960, looking north towards Portland Terrace and the Civic Centre, seen through the newly created opening for the inner ring road in the town's ancient walls, with the steps leading up to Arundel Tower on the left. *(Eric Thompson Collection – Bitterne Local History Society)*

The former cul-de-sac Portland Terrace is now an important ring road, and an ultra-modern bridge replaces the gap in the town's former defences to provide a scenic walkway along the walls for tourists. *(Jim Brown)*

Forest View *c.*1895. The terraced properties in Weymouth Terrace can be seen in the distance. The walkway along the shore was constructed in 1850 with access via the well-known '40 Steps' at the end of Forest View. *(Henry Brain Collection – Maureen Webber)*

Western Esplanade (*c.*1908) has now been enhanced by trees, and the Power Station, which was constructed in 1903, is clearly visible. This supplied the power for the town's new electric tram cars. *(Eric Thompson Collection – Bitterne Local History Society)*

Western Esplanade, *c.*1977, again from Forest View but now with a clear view of the Pirelli office buildings and Arundel Towers office blocks. The rounded top of the Centre Inn at the bottom of Bargate Street is visible behind the old walls. *(Eric Thompson Collection – Bitterne Local History Society)*

The large Marks & Spencer store section of the West Quay development has now blocked Western Esplanade but access is still possible via the '40 Steps' in the foreground or steps leading from Bargate Street. *(Matt McManus)*

Western Esplanade *c.*1855. Looking south one can see the newly constructed '40 Steps' giving access from the town to the shoreline. In the background is West Quay from where the Pilgrim Fathers sailed in 1620. *(Jim Brown)*

Western Esplanade (*c.*1890) has now been surfaced and allows vehicular access to Pickett's Boatyard opposite the Westgate. Forest View, from where the New Forest was clearly visible, was developed in 1880. *(Eric Gadd)*

Western Esplanade *c*.1948. Viewed from the top of West Gate, the public mortuary and ambulance station are obscured by the advert hoardings, with Pirelli General Cable Works in the background. St Michael's Lodging House is on the right. *(Eric Thompson Collection – Bitterne Local History Society)*

The De Vere Hotel complex and the New Baths now dominate the foreground, and Western Esplanade is now a cul-de-sac, blocked by the West Quay development. St Michael's Lodging House no longer exists. *(Jim Brown)*

Bugle Street *c*.1895. The early 16th-century Tudor House was the home of Sir Richard Lyster, Lord Chief Justice of the King's Bench in 1546–52, but was divided into separate lodgings and businesses when this picture was taken. *(Cobwebs Collection – Peter Boyd-Smith)*

The house and grounds were bought by William Spranger in 1886, and he spent a considerable sum restoring it before selling it to Southampton Corporation in 1911 for less than his outlay. It is now a fine museum. *(Jim Brown)*

Bugle Street, *c.*1975, looking south from Simnel Street with Tudor House on the south-west corner of Blue Anchor Lane (called Wytegod's Lane in the early mediaeval period). The derelict site was formerly St Michael's Lodging House. *(Genevieve Bailey)*

The earlier fine view of the north face of Tudor House is now obscured by a modern housing development, but this has a good visual appeal and fits in very well indeed with the area's former mediaeval status. *(Jim Brown)*

The houses in Simnel Street and the surrounding area behind the town's ancient walls were cramped and without proper sanitation. It was here that the town's first slum clearance started in the mid-1890s. *(Left: Eric Gadd*, Right: *Jim Brown)*

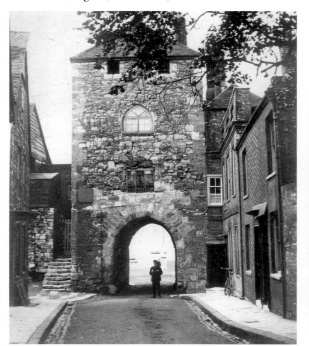

Henry V marched through the West Gate to his triumph at Agincourt in 1415 and the Pilgrim fathers to their 'New World' in 1620. The area is now reclaimed and hotels stand where ships once moored. *(Left: Henry Brain Collection – Maureen Webber*, Right: *Jim Brown)*

Western Docks, *c.*1934, looking west across the newly constructed quayside with the reclaimed ground yet to have Rank's Flour Mill. RMS *Mauretania* is in the far distance and in the foreground are the Mayflower and Stella Memorials. *(Cobwebs Collection – Peter Boyd-Smith)*

The Herbert Walker Avenue entrance to the Docks via Gate 8 is now restricted and the former waste ground either side of West Quay Road is highly industrialised, together with several varied entertainment facilities. *(Jim Brown)*

Western Docks, *c.*1948, showing No.8 Dock Gate leading to Herbert Walker Avenue with an unmade road across the waste reclaimed ground. Rank's Flour Mill can be seen in the distance behind temporary industrial buildings. *(Eric Thompson Collection – Bitterne Local History Society)*

The former track is now West Quay Road, a major route to the west. The Holiday Inn, originally called The Skyways then Post House, dominates the skyline, with the De Vere Grand Harbour hotel on the right. *(Jim Brown)*

Brunswick Square, *c.*1956, leading off Bridge Street, now Bernard Street. This once fashionable mid-Victorian square suffered bomb damage in World War Two and was consequently neglected. The demolition team is now about to move in! *(Eric Thompson Collection – Bitterne Local History Society)*

Post-war development resulted in the removal of all the square's residential properties, thus enabling the businesses in adjacent Queensway to extend at their rear into what is now a common service area. *(Jim Brown)*

Bridge Street *c.*1850. The Clarendon Family Hotel on the corner of Orchard Place is boasting of its hot and cold vapour and shower baths. It became the Glasgow Hotel in the 1880s when it was owned by Cooper's Brewery. *(Jim Brown)*

St Michael's and Holy Rood Church spires are still in the background in this photograph taken *c.*1908. On the right is one of the Misselbrook & Weston's chain of grocery stores at No.20, opened in 1886 by Frederick Misselbrook. *(Eric Gadd)*

Bernard Street *c.*1945, formerly named Bridge Street (renamed in 1924). The Glasgow Hotel was destroyed by enemy action in 1940 and the site is derelict in this photograph. The Holy Rood Church spire also vanished in the bombing. *(Eric Thompson Collection – Bitterne Local History Society)*

Large blocks of flats now occupy the site of the former shops, and the Glasgow Hotel, rebuilt in 1958, was re-opened as Dixie's in 1990. The building is now Martin's Rubber Co. Ltd, established in 1865. *(Jim Brown)*

Platform Road *c.*1903. The old Custom House, built in 1902, was adjacent to Dock Gate 4 and opposite Queens Park. It was an impressive building for its time as HM Customs Officers were a very important part of the port's life. *(Henry Brain Collection – Maureen Webber)*

The advent of the European Community and significant changes in border controls has meant a scaling down of HM Customs staff, who have now relocated. The rebuilt Portcullis House is currently unoccupied. *(Jim Brown)*

Canute Road *c.*1865. The Sailors' Home was established in 1861 next to the nautical equipment premises of Joseph R. Stebbing, Mayor in 1867 and the main promoter of the Hartley Institute, now Southampton University. *(Eric Gadd)*

The Sailors' Home moved to nearby Oxford Street in 1909, and after years of use by shipping agents the site became home to the BTC Sports Club, now demolished and to be developed into apartments. *(Jim Brown)*

Canute Road *c.*1975. On the right is the imposing office block of Dock House, the headquarters of the dock owners, the British Transport Docks Board, who managed a very large labour force of dock workers during this period. *(Eric Thompson Collection – Bitterne Local History Society)*

The renamed Associated British Ports no longer manage a labour force, and Dock House has been relocated and replaced by luxury apartments. Ocean Village, in the distance, was formerly a busy working dock area. *(Jim Brown)*

The rear of Terminus Station *c.*1975. The railway lines catered for the boat and freight trains leading directly into the Docks across Canute Road. In the background are the large warehouses and vehicles of the New Zealand Shipping Company. *(Eric Thompson Collection – Bitterne Local History Society)*

The railway lines have been reduced to a single track but they still afford occasional access to the Docks. Apartment blocks, mainly catering for University students, have replaced the area's warehousing function. *(Jim Brown)*

Eastern Docks, *c*.1975, taken from the roof of the former South Western Hotel, now converted into luxury apartments, which shows the busy and diverse nature of this part of the docks during this period. (*Eric Thompson Collection – Bitterne Local History Society*)

This section of the Eastern Docks is now almost entirely devoted to serving the car import/export trade, but in the background is the *Queen Elizabeth II* on Berths 38/39, next to a large car transporter vessel. (*Jim Brown*)

Floating Bridge Road *c.*1948. Tram passengers travelling to and from Woolston have a direct connection with the Floating Bridge, and the Popular Café can just be seen on the corner of Bridge Terrace. Canute Road is on the right in the background. *(Cobwebs Collection – Peter Boyd-Smith)*

The front area of the old road is now submerged under the new road linking the Central Bridge with the Itchen Bridge, and it is no longer possible to take a photograph from exactly the same position. *(Jim Brown)*

St Mary Street *c.*1897. The Kingsland Tavern on the left dates back to the early 1820s and was taken over by Brickwood's Brewery in 1925. The flags are almost certainly out for Queen Victoria's Diamond Jubilee. *(Henry Brain Collection – Maureen Webber)*

The Kingsland Tavern is still an important asset to the local community, which continues to thrive while anticipating major changes to its structure as a result of a large regeneration grant awarded recently. *(Jim Brown)*

Kingsland Square *c.*1930. This ancient, well-patronised open air market was always a much loved focal point for the local working-class residents. South Front, with its terraced houses and Primitive Methodist church, is in the background. *(Eric Thompson Collection – Bitterne Local History Society)*

The market is now greatly reduced in size but is still well attended by a growing local population. New apartments can be seen on the left, and South Front is now obscured by the modern St Mary's Surgery. *(Jim Brown)*

Orchard Lane *c*.1948. Lime Street is on the left and the entrance to Bell Street can just be seen on the right. This was a bustling down-town area with a number of second-hand clothing and furniture shops catering to local demand. *(Eric Thompson Collection – Bitterne Local History Society)*

Multi-storey Council flats replaced the many small local shops in 1958, and the area, although immediately adjoining the large number of shops and stores in nearby East Street, is now completely residential. *(Jim Brown)*

Northam Road *c.*1900. The Glebe Hotel on the corner of Northam and Brintons Roads dates back to the 1870s. In 1988 it was painted bright mauve and pink and called the Queen Vic, named after the pub in a popular TV series. *(Cobwebs Collection – Peter Boyd-Smith)*

Repainted battleship grey in 1994 and called the Gaol House, the pub is now freshly painted cream and renamed the King Alfred. It serves a popular area full of antique shops on what is now in a cul-de-sac. *(Jim Brown)*

Northam Road *c.*1974. The tower block of Clifford House dominates the scene immediately behind the Six Dials roundabout, a convergence of St Mary Street with New, St Andrews, St Mary's, St Marks and Northam Roads. *(Eric Thompson Collection – Bitterne Local History Society)*

Clifford House has been demolished and replaced by the Premier Travel Inn. The Six Dials no longer exists and the buildings on the right have been given a new frontage, with the end of the terrace being demolished. *(Jim Brown)*

St Marks Road, *c.*1976, taken from the top of St Mary Street, looking down with Nichols Road in the distance. Corke's Radio shop premises are on the right corner at the junction with St Marks Road and Northam Road. *(Eric Thompson Collection – Bitterne Local History Society)*

The junction has been completely transformed; Corke's Radio has been demolished to help create a pedestrian tunnel leading to Brintons Road and Nichols Road, and Northam Road is now a cul-de-sac. *(Jim Brown)*

St Marks Road, *c.*1976, taken from Nichols Road at the junction with Brintons Road. The Bridge Tavern can be seen at the Six Dials end of St Marks Road with the tower block of Clifford House to its far right. *(Eric Thompson Collection – Bitterne Local History Society)*

The 172-bed Premier Travel Inn that replaced Clifford House is obscured by the large apartment block that has been constructed on the site of the former block of houses in the now vanished St Marks Road. *(Jim Brown)*

St Mary's Road, photographed *c.1976*, used to join St Mary Street at the well-known Six Dials junction, but by this period it had been truncated as part of a gyratory system. In 1874 the SPQR furniture store was a Bible Christian chapel. *(Eric Thompson Collection – Bitterne Local History Society)*

St Mary's Road is now even more truncated and not visible from the former St Marks Road junction. Both are covered by the dual carriageway leading to Northam Bridge, and Six Dials no longer exists. *(Jim Brown)*

Northam Road *c*.1950. The Wonder Inn at No.182 on the corner of York Street (formerly known as Paradise Row) opened in 1855 and closed in 1958. It was named after an old Southampton/Channel Island paddle steamer. *(Cobwebs Collection – Peter Boyd-Smith)*

The public house was demolished when the district was developed, making room for an open area in front of the parade of shops. The multi-storey Millbank House overlooks this neighbourhood of Council properties. *(Jim Brown)*

Northam Road, *c.*1909, looking east. The Engineer's Arms at No.98 (its first landlord is thought to have been an engine driver) dates back to the 1850s and can be seen on the corner of Wilson Street. It closed in 1982. *(Cobwebs Collection – Peter Boyd-Smith)*

The former public house is now a dental laboratory, and high-rise Millbank House rears up from the former working-class area of Prince's Street. Traffic lights are necessary to cater for the nearby 'Saints' stadium. *(Matt McManus)*

Mount Pleasant *c.*1900. The Mount Pleasant railway crossing can barely be seen in this poor quality but rare picture of the timber ponds just west of Northam Bridge. The author also jumped from log to log long before he could swim! *(Henry Brain Collection – Maureen Webber)*

The securing posts at the outer extremity of the former timber ponds can still be seen even though most of the area was reclaimed when the Southern Television studios expanded north of the former Plaza cinema. *(Jim Brown)*

Northam Bridge *c*.1953. Work has started on the new concrete bridge, but the old cast-iron bridge is still in use. On the left is the 2,100-seat Plaza Cinema, opened in 1932 but closed in 1957 and replaced by Southern Television studios. *(Eric Thompson Collection – Bitterne Local History Society)*

The renamed Meridian TV have now vacated their studios and moved to Whiteley, and the road leading to the 1889 bridge is now a cul-de-sac. An automatic camera currently polices the Northam Road traffic lights. *(Matt McManus)*

Cobden Bridge, photographed *c.*1905, opened in 1883. This bridge was built by the National Liberal Land Company who gave it to the town having bought and developed 317 acres of adjacent farmland to the east that they called Bitterne Park. *(Jim Brown)*

The replacement concrete bridge was built in 1928 at a cost of £45,000, and apartment blocks have appeared on both sides of the river. Dyers Boatyard, visible on the St Denys side, remains a popular local amenity. *(Jim Brown)*

Chapel Street *c.*1905, so called because of its three Chapels: the Wesleyan (in the background), Congregational (now United Reformed) and Baptist (later Anglican). This photograph was taken from outside the Congregational Church. *(Bitterne Local History Society)*

The site of the Congregational Church is now on the centre island of the bypass, but the remaining realigned and truncated section of Chapel Street, renamed Dean Road in 1924, can be seen in the background. *(Jim Brown)*

Bitterne Road *c.1979*. 'Sports', selling a wide range of bicycles, is at the top of Lances Hill, with the horse trough outside as a memento of the days when horse-drawn vehicles needed a break after travelling up the steep hill. *(Bitterne Local History Society)*

By 1985, when the bypass was completed, this part of the busy Bitterne Road leading to Portsmouth had been transformed into a thriving precinct. 'Sports' is now an abandoned former vegetable and fruit shop. *(Matt McManus)*

The building on the corner of Pound Street and Bitterne Road was originally the site of Southwell's Dairy, but Lloyds Bank has been there since 1932, from the days when Bitterne was still a village, photographed c.1982. *(Bitterne Local History Society)*

Now Lloyds TSB, the bank continues to be an important part of the local scene, and although the parade of shops have changed owners many times they are basically unchanged, creating the popular precinct. *(Matt McManus)*

Bitterne Road in 1976 showing Guster's at No.436, just before it closed in March 1976. Harry Guster's Ironmongers shop first opened in 1950 near the top of Lances Hill and later moved to this spot on what had been Bitterne Motor Works. *(Eric Thompson Collection – Bitterne Local History Society)*

A block of shops surmounted by the United Reformed Church, relocated from its former position on the corner of Dean Road, now occupy the site. Bursledon Road now ends at what was the 'Bitterne Fork'. *(Matt McManus)*

Bitterne Road *c.*1935. This stretch of shops and flats was called Bitterne Parade but the name was removed during World War Two for security reasons and never replaced. It lay empty and neglected for many years. *(Bitterne Local History Society)*

Problems with the absentee landlord were eventually solved and recent extensive alterations to the roof have dramatically improved it. It is now a popular store stocking a wide variety of DIY and garden products. *(Jim Brown)*

Bursledon Road *c*.1980. Albert Terrace, opposite Bitterne Church Tennis Courts, was home to a number of old Bitterne families and was built in 1851. The Red Lion public house and the entrance to Red Lion Cut can just be seen on the left. *(Bitterne Local History Society)*

The entire terrace was demolished in 1982 for the construction of the bypass, and just beyond the parked cars is a very busy dual carriageway 'protected' by speed cameras, out of sight around a bend! *(Jim Brown)*

Bursledon Road *c.1975*. A closer view of Red Lion Cut with part of Bitterne Drill Hall, rebuilt around 1910, on the left corner. Destruction of one of the terraced cottages by vandals has started, but the remainder were left until 1982. *(Eric Thompson Collection – Bitterne Local History Society)*

Red Lion Cut and the Drill Hall have now vanished completely, but the Red Lion public house is still there. The car sale premises were subsequently rebuilt and behind them is a large Tiles R Us showroom. *(Matt McManus)*

Red Lion Cut *c.*1975. Bitterne's original Drill Hall was replaced around 1910 by this substantial building as a base for the Hampshire 1st Volunteer Brigade of the Royal Artillery. It also served as a fire station in World War Two. *(Bitterne Local History Society)*

The Drill Hall site and former Red Lion Cut now serves as the car park for the Tiles R Us showroom, just out of sight on the left, and this stretch of Bitterne Road has been turned into a pedestrian underpass. *(Matt McManus)*

Bitterne Road, *c.*1982, looking down towards the Red Lion fork and top of Lances Hill. The Bitterne lion is barely visible on the roof of Lion Place, on the left is an advert for the Hampshire Pet Centre and Poodle Parlour on its wall. *(Bitterne Local History Society)*

The stretch of Bitterne Road containing Lion Place has been completely obliterated and it now sweeps right to join Maybray King Way en route to town. Tiles R Us now occupies the space behind the Red Lion pub. *(Jim Brown)*

Upper Deacon Road *c.*1910. Originally called Furzey Lane then Thornhill Road, this view is facing Thornhill and the crossing with Bursledon Road, also known as 'Sheep Wash' from when sheep were driven here to Southampton market. *(Bitterne Local History Society)*

The crossroad has now been realigned for safety reasons and protected by traffic lights, as are so many of Southampton's junctions! The former strawberry fields and brickyards have been replaced by housing. *(Jim Brown)*

Bassett Avenue *c.*1879. John Pragnell, the Turnpike Toll Collector, aged 30 and living with his wife and three children at the Mission Room, Burgess Street, waits for traffic at the top of Bassett Avenue near the Red Lodge Nursery. *(Norman Gardiner Collection – Bitterne Local History Society)*

John Pragnell would earn a small fortune in commission from the almost continuous traffic using the widened Bassett Avenue today, much of it originating from the nearby M3 motorway. *(Jim Brown)*

Mayfield Road in 1912. E.H. Cox, General Grocer, on the corner of Woodcote Road is boldly advertising both Fry's and Cadbury's chocolate in the shop window. It is most likely Mrs Cox who is standing in the doorway. *(Norman Gardiner Collection – Bitterne Local History Society)*

As is sadly only too often the case, the demise of the small shopkeeper serving the local community has given the developer another opportunity to convert the building to residential use. *(Jim Brown)*

Burgess Street, *c.*1909, looking down to the junction with Langhorn Road on the right. The road continues as far as the junction with Portswood Road/High Road. This peaceful view shows the rural nature of the area at this period. *(Norman Gardiner Collection – Bitterne Local History Society)*

Renamed Burgess Road in 1924, the area was developed by the Swaythling Housing Society in the late 1920s. Swaythling Methodist Church was built in the former field in 1932 and still serves the area well. *(Jim Brown)*

High Road, *c.*1905, looking north, with several good quality semi-detached private properties and a traffic-free unmade track. Trees at the junction with the then narrow Burgess Street on the far left make it appear to be a cul-de-sac. *(Norman Gardiner Collection – Bitterne Local History Society)*

The Victorian houses have been replaced by Colley's Supper Rooms at No.51, followed by several small shops and culminating with the ubiquitous McDonald's restaurant on the corner with Burgess Road. *(Jim Brown)*

High Road *c.*1905. Henry John Baker's grocery store on the corner of Fleming Road is serving the local Swaythling residents, whose children can play in the street in safety with little to fear from the sparse, non-motorised traffic. *(Norman Gardiner Collection – Bitterne Local History Society)*

The former grocery shop is now a Chinese & Thai Food Takeaway, and the former private houses are now shop premises, including another Chinese Takeaway! The road is now too busy for children to play there. *(Jim Brown)*

Burgess Street *c.*1900. Built *c.*1871, the Bassett Hotel was once famous for its gardens and amusements for both adults and children, including a bear pit containing real bears! Boxing matches were also held at this popular venue. *(Henry Brain Collection- Maureen Webber)*

This picture was taken in January 2005, just prior to its closure, and the small inset view the following April, shows how quickly developers move! The large site will provide considerable private accommodation. *(Jim Brown)*

Portswood Road *c*.1950. Mrs M.S. Gaiger's drapers shop at No. 573 stands on the corner of Brickfield Road and further along is the Newlands Hotel, known as the New Inn in 1803. The name change occurred in the 1920s. *(Bitterne Local History Society)*

The useful drapers shop has been replaced by housing and the Newlands, as it was then known, closed in 1991. It suffered a serious arson attack the following year and was consequently replaced by a block of flats. *(Jim Brown)*

Burgess Road in 1928, looking towards Swaythling, while the last tramway extension from The Junction to Bassett and Portswood was being laid. Miss Longster's bungalow and nursery is on the left. *(Norman Gardiner Collection – Bitterne Local History Society)*

Trams have been replaced by buses and Burgess Court Old People's Home built on the site of the nursery. The adjacent library, built at a cost of £7,850, opened on 22 May 1935 with an initial stock of 6,000 volumes. *(Jim Brown)*

University Road in 1924, taken during the visit of HRH the Prince of Wales to the University on 27 June. The Stile Inn on the corner of Burgess Road dates from the 1860s and was destroyed in an arson attack in 1990. *(Norman Gardiner Collection – Bitterne Local History Society)*

The houses have been replaced by University buildings. The rebuilt Stiles, catering for the local large student population, was once called the Hedgehog and Hogshead and brewed its own beer. *(Jim Brown)*

The new building of University College in what was originally called Back Lane, photographed *c.*1918. It was opened in May 1914 but was instantly taken over by the War Department as a Military Hospital and not released until 1919. *(Norman Gardiner Collection – Bitterne Local History Society)*

Back Lane is now University Road, and the College is the University of Southampton. The one or two hundred students from its very early days have now increased to over 20,000 within eight faculties. *(Jim Brown)*

Salisbury Road *c.*1980. This road appears in the 1899 local street directory with only four houses and ran from what was then Church Lane in Highfield. The area changed in character when the University College appeared in 1914. *(Norman Gardiner Collection – Bitterne Local History Society)*

Further wide sweeping changes have now taken place and all the properties have been demolished. The former terrace of Salisbury Road now gives access to a large car park serving the popular Nuffield Theatre. *(Jim Brown)*

Portswood Road *c.*1905. A horse bus is passing the Brook Inn at 466 Portswood Road on the corner of Belgrave Road. The public house dates back to the 1860s and was shown as a beer house on the 1878 Southampton Drink Map. *(Henry Brain Collection – Maureen Webber)*

Now known as merely The Brook, the public house serves a much larger local population as well as being on a much busier highway, which also serves a large B&Q warehouse further up on the left, out of sight. *(Jim Brown)*

Another view of the Brook Inn, this time from the north, *c.*1950, with a small cluster of houses known as Brook Terrace just ahead of the junction with Belgrave Road. 'Omo' washing powder is no longer advertised! (*Bitterne Local History Society*)

Brook Terrace has been replaced by a car sales showroom and The Brook is considerably enlarged from its original construction. It also boasts conspicuous graffiti specially commissioned in 1993 in the bar. (*Jim Brown*)

Portswood Road *c.*1980. Trams were first built here by Southampton Corporation in 1908 and were replaced by buses in 1950. This picture of the bus depot offices, behind which buses were parked, was taken just prior to its demolition. *(Eric Thompson Collection – Bitterne Local History Society)*

Although still used as a parking area for the city buses, with much smaller office accommodation, the site is currently under consideration for development, possibly becoming a supermarket, with the depot relocated. *(Jim Brown)*

Onslow Road *c.*1910. The imposing Wesleyan Methodist Chapel on the corner of Peterborough Road was built in 1858 after a leading Methodist, William Betts, sold his Bevois Mount Estate, of which this was a part, for development. *(Norman Gardiner Collection – Bitterne Local History Society)*

The Wesleyan Chapel was sold in 1962 to the well regarded local Sikh community and is their Gurdwara Nanaksar Temple. Peterborough Road is now a cul-de-sac, and the shops on the right were replaced by car showrooms. *(Jim Brown)*

Hill Lane *c*.1950. Jack Buck's garage on the corner of Burgess Road was also agent for the now rare Morris, Wolseley and Standard cars, as well as being a petrol station (where customers were not allowed to serve themselves). *(Eric Thompson Collection – Bitterne Local History Society)*

The garage is now a Somerfield Food Store, and the two former adjacent crossroads with Winchester and Burgess Roads are extremely busy double roundabouts. *(Jim Brown)*

Winchester Road *c.1957*. The 'Children's Hospital and Dispensary for Women' was established in Church Street, Shirley, in 1884 and moved to these purpose-built premises in 1912, where children received sympathetic and caring treatment. *(Eric Thompson Collection – Bitterne Local History Society)*

Hospital reorganisation in 1974 resulted in the expert staff and facilities transferring to the nearby General Hospital in Tremona Road. The building was demolished in 1982 and the site redeveloped for housing. *(Jim Brown)*

Church Street *c.*1910. The owner and staff of H. Hicks, bakers and confectioners in Shirley, stand proudly outside their shop at No.37, with their new looking delivery carriages neatly parked up outside the flour store. *(Cobwebs Collection – Peter Boyd-Smith)*

Both the shop and much of the adjoining terrace of houses have now been swept away to provide the entrance to Vincent Road, leading to the large block of Council flats in the background. *(Jim Brown)*

Shirley High Street, *c*.1902, looking east, with Anglesea Road on the left. The Queen Victoria Jubilee Fountain on the right was erected in 1889 outside the Salisbury Arms, which was built in the 1860s on the corner of Newman Street. *(Cobwebs Collection – Peter Boyd-Smith)*

The Jubilee Fountain was moved to the opposite side of the road in 1923 and re-erected in 1976 in the new shopping precinct on the left, where a new, large Sainsbury store has recently been built. *(Jim Brown)*

Park Street *c.*1975. Lowther's Garage dominates the upper section of Park Street, leading to Shirley High Street. The houses on the left end at the junction with Carlisle Road, where the Shirley Corporation Bus Depot is located. *(Eric Thompson Collection – Bitterne Local History Society)*

Kwik-Fit now occupies part of the Lowther's Garage premises, with the remainder replaced by a block of private apartments. Shirley Corporation Bus Depot is no more, having been replaced with housing. *(Jim Brown)*

Shirley High Street *c.*1903. On the right, at the corner with Church Street, is the large boot and shoe store of William Gange. Tram No. 40 has travelled from Prospect Place on the town's first electric route, opened only three years earlier. *(Bill Moore)*

Trams were completely superseded by buses by 1950, and William Gange is now a Mackays Store. Very few, if any, of the shops and stores have retained their original owners in this thriving city suburb. *(Jim Brown)*

Shirley Road *c.*1950. Emanuel, goldsmith, watchmaker and jeweller, heads the terrace of shops next door to the well-known sports outfitters Holt & Haskell. In the background is St Boniface's Roman Catholic Church, built in 1927. *(Bill Moore)*

Holt & Haskell's and the church have survived, but the vast majority of the other shops have changed hands. Arthur Holt was a Hampshire County cricketer and Reg Haskell, a former Mayor of Southampton. *(Jim Brown)*

North East Road in 2002. This Sholing Salvation Army Hall was opened in August 1928, but, although it had served the community well, it was in urgent need of expensive refurbishment and was demolished in 2002. *(Jim Brown)*

Completed by March 2003, the new building possesses the latest facilities including modern kitchen equipment and electronic visual/sound systems, together with a greatly increased seating capacity. *(Jim Brown)*

South East Road in 1998. Percy and Arthur Russell started this popular ironmongery store with their demob money in 1946, following their discharge from the army. Originally only a small section, it eventually expanded to the above extent. (*Jim Brown*)

After the death of Percy in 1989, preceded by that of Arthur, the business was managed by Percy's son Robert, but in 1998 the family sold out to the adjacent Allday's store. It was later taken over by the Co-op. (*Jim Brown*)

Kathleen Road in 2001. Robert Russell then continued as the local ironmonger and builder's merchant by moving down to the junction with Kathleen Road, also diversifying into garden products at the rear. *(Jim Brown)*

Developers found the spot appealing and by 2002 took over the site to build pleasant housing. However, all the products formerly stocked by Russells are still available at John's DIY in nearby Botany Bay Road. *(Matt McManus)*

South East Road *c.*1915. Alf and Will Parker tend to their horses on the orchard and strawberry fields owned by their father, James, at the junction with Butts Road. Strawberries were a prominent feature of the Sholing area at this time. *(Jim Brown)*

Strawberries and the orchard have been replaced by housing and St Andrew's Methodist Church, which was opened on 29 November 1969 by Dr Horace King, Speaker of the House of Commons and later Lord Maybray-King. *(Jim Brown)*

Bishops Road in 1998. Ken Lamper's bakery was started at No.37 in 1939 by his father, Ernie, when it was only a small building. Ken and his wife Shirley are standing outside their family business after taking a well-earned retirement. *(Jim Brown)*

Developers bought the site and converted what had been a well respected and admired family business into good quality housing. The demise of such small but popular businesses is sadly all too common these days. *(Jim Brown)*

North East Road in 2000, and Tom McEniry's The Happy Shopper at No.19 after he retired following 30 years' service to the area. Such small shops served a real need in the community, especially for the elderly, and they are sorely missed. (*Jim Brown*)

The relentless march of the developer has resulted in yet another small business being replaced by housing. However, the former shop and its spacious garden have now provided several good quality properties. (*Jim Brown*)

Spring Road, *c.1900*, looking south from the direction of Peartree Avenue, with two young men standing at the junction with Blackthorn Road to their right. This clearly shows the rural nature of Merry Oak during this period. *(Bitterne Local History Society)*

The 51 acres of the Merry Oak estate were purchased by the Corporation in 1928, and the building of 616 houses began the following year. A stipulation for the developers was that many of the trees had to remain. *(Matt McManus)*

Weston Lane, *c.*1905, and the lower of two arches erected by William Chamberlayne so he could ride his carriages across both parts of his estate, after he built Weston Grove House in 1802. The Sun Hotel is shown just beyond the arch. *(Henry Brain Collection – Maureen Webber)*

The arch was demolished in 1948 but the remnants of the left-hand approach earth banks are still visible. The Sun Hotel, which dated from the early 1830s, is now closed and awaiting redevelopment. *(Jim Brown)*

Weston Lane *c.*1905. Mayfield House was built *c.*1856 on part of the large Chamberlayne Estate and was sold to Lord Radstock in 1889. The upper arch completed the circuit and was also used by his Lordship's carriages. *(Henry Brain Collection – Maureen Webber)*

The arch was demolished in 1931 and Mayfield sold to Southampton Corporation in 1937. It now remains a public pleasure park. On the right is the entrance to the fine Chamberlayne Leisure Centre, built in 2000. *(Jim Brown)*

Portsmouth Road *c.*1956. A very useful selection of bus stops was available for passengers coming off the floating bridges. The Cliff Hotel, to the right and dating back to the 1830s, was the home of the Southampton Rhythm Club. *(Norman Gardiner Collection – Bitterne Local History Society)*

With the construction of the Itchen Bridge in 1977, the area underwent a dramatic transformation with new housing replacing the former bus shelters. The Cliff Hotel closed in the late 1980s and is now apartments. *(Matt McManus)*

Another view of the floating bridge bus station *c.*1956, this time looking west along Portsmouth Road. Edward Green's popular coffee rooms are visible on the right, at the junction with Hazel and Oakbank Roads. *(Norman Gardiner Collection – Bitterne Local History Society)*

Taken on a Sunday morning with the shops closed, this normally busy area looks peaceful. The preserved chain propulsion system section of the fondly remembered Floating Bridge can be seen in the background. *(Matt McManus)*

Portsmouth Road *c.*1900. On the right, on the corner of Bridge Road, are the premises of William Henry Bell, solicitor and clerk to the Itchen Urban District Council. Further down is an advert of D. Chill, pawnbroker and jeweller. *(Norman Gardiner Collection – Bitterne Local History Society)*

What became the offices of Bell, Pope and Bridgewater, 3 Bridge Road, were destroyed in 1940, and the site has not been built on. The floating bridges, visible in 1900, were replaced by the Itchen Bridge in 1977. *(Matt McManus)*

Looking east along Portsmouth Road *c.*1908, with St Mary's Presbyterian Church on the corner of John's Road. The nearby tall gabled building is the Corn Exchange, owned by Gamble & Chalk, corn and coal merchants. *(Eric Thompson Collection – Bitterne Local History Society)*

St Mary's Presbytarian Church has been replaced by the Co-op supermarket, and all the shops, including the Corn Market, have now changed hands. The former dental surgery on the extreme right is now a bank. *(Matt McManus)*

Bridge Road in 1973 looking south west from Woolston railway footbridge in October; one can see Lower Vicarage Road running directly alongside the bridge passing over Bridge Road, with Oak Bank Road to its left. (*Eric Thompson Collection – Bitterne Local History Society*)

By March 1974 both roads had vanished in preparation for the construction of the Itchen Bridge, and the River Itchen is now visible in the background, as well as the rear of premises in lower Portsmouth Road. (*Eric Thompson Collection – Bitterne Local History Society*)

By July 1975 preparations are well under way, with sections of the new Itchen Bridge visible in the background and the concrete supports to bridge Bridge Road partially complete in the left foreground. *(Eric Thompson Collection – Bitterne Local History Society)*

The railway signal semaphore arm has been removed, and the massive Itchen Bridge obscures the former view, stretching across the river to a town that now has a totally different skyline.
(Matt McManus)

Oakbank Road, *c.*1972, taken from the junction with Hazel Road. The shop premises of Woolston Handicrafts Wool Shop at No. 13 are on the corner of Laurel Road. Further along, just out of sight, is the Ebenezer Gospel Hall. *(Eric Thompson Collection – Bitterne Local History Society)*

The Itchen Bridge construction completely obliterated the properties in both Oakbank and Laurel Roads. The area is now used for lorry and car parking, as well as remaining an access to Bridge Road. *(Matt McManus)*

A view of the rear of the properties in Oakbank Road in 1973, taken from the top of the earthworks thrown up during the construction of the Itchen Bridge. The Vosper Thornycroft sheds are visible in the background. *(Eric Thompson Collection – Bitterne Local History Society)*

The car park at the rear of the Portsmouth Road shops has replaced the Oakbank Road houses, and there is now no trace of Laurel Road. Most of the Vosper Thornycroft sheds have also now disappeared. *(Matt McManus)*

Bridge Road in 1974. In January work started on the eastern end of the new Itchen Bridge, and the premises of G. Peters & Co., wine & spirit merchants, and Cluett Burns, commercial stationers, are being demolished. *(Eric Thompson Collection – Bitterne Local History Society)*

By March that year the ground has been cleared and the wall of the Boat Shop, selling a very wide variety of boating equipment and sundries at the end of The Colonnade, is under repair. *(Eric Thompson Collection – Bitterne Local History Society)*

By July 1975 the Boat Shop is once again fully operational, and the process of constructing a further bridge across Bridge Road is well under way. The damaged road surface, however, still has to be made up. *(Eric Thompson Collection – Bitterne Local History Society)*

The Boat Shop is now the Boat Shop Café, and the Post Office has relocated into The Colonnade from its former position in Portsmouth Road. The Itchen Bridge is now an established part of Woolston. *(Jim Brown)*

Lower Vicarage Road, *c.*1950, looking across the River Itchen and showing the tall and derelict Supermarine Aviation Works administration and drawing offices in Hazel Road that were destroyed in the air raids of September 1940. *(Bitterne Local History Society)*

There is no trace of the former grand Supermarine complex from Lower Vicarage Road, now a cul-de-sac, and high-rise offices on the town side of the river have dramatically changed the skyline. *(Jim Brown)*

Woodley Road in 1975 taken from Keswick Road and looking towards Portsmouth Road, with the Woolston Picture House, opened in 1913, in the background. The small off-licence on the left corner was a popular amenity. *(Eric Thompson Collection – Bitterne Local History Society)*

Most of the houses have been swept away to provide free car parking facilities, and the Woolston Picture House is now a bingo hall. A health clinic has also been built, just out of view, to the left of the picture. *(Matt McManus)*

Vosper Thornycroft in 2003. HMS *Mersey*, an off-shore patrol vessel, was the last Royal Navy ship to be built at the Vosper Thornycroft yard, an era that started when John I. Thornycroft came to Woolston in 1904 and ended in 2004. *(Jim Brown)*

The site is now almost cleared for a final dramatic change to one of Southampton's faces. Vosper Thornycroft has relocated to Portsmouth and a £350 million redevelopment housing scheme is now under consideration. *(Jim Brown)*

INDEX

Above Bar Street 22–29
Upper Above Bar 30–31
Albion Place 73
Arundel Tower 72
Back Lane 124
Bargate 18, 20, 21
Bargate Street 19
Bassett Avenue 115
Bedford Place 44
Bernard Street 85
Bishops Road 141
Bitterne Road 106–109, 113
Bridge Road 150–151, 154–155
Bridge Street 84
Brunswick Place 36–37
Brunswick Square 83
Bugle Street 78, 79
Burgess Street (Road) 117, 120, 122
Burlington Road 59
Bursledon Road 110–111
Burton Road 57
Canute Road 87, 88
Chapel Street 105
Church Street 132
Civic Centre Road 49–50, 52–53
Cobden Bridge 104
Commercial Road 51, 55
Dean Road 105
East Park Terr. 38
East Street 13–14
Eastern Docks 90
Floating Bridge Road 91
Forest View 74
Havelock Road 54
High Road 118–119
High Street 12
High Street, (Lower) 5
High Street, (Centre) 6–7
High Street, (Upper) 8–11, 16, 17
Hill Lane 130
Junction 32–35
Kathleen Road 139
Kingsland Square 93

London Road 40–43
Lower Vicarage Road 156
Maddison Street 63
Marlands House 51
Mayfield Road 116
Millbrook Road 60
Milton Road 58
Mount Pleasant 102
North East Road 137, 142
Northam Bridge 103
Northam Road 95–96, 100–101
Oakbank Road 152–153
Onslow Road 129
Orchard Lane 94
Park Street 134
Platform Road 86
Polygon 56
Portland Terrace 64–68, 70
Portsmouth Road 146–149
Portswood Road 121, 126–128
Post House (from top) 61
Red Lion Cut 112
Salisbury Road 125
Shirley High Street 133, 135
Shirley Road 136
Simnel Street 80
South East Road 138, 140
Spring Road 143
St Marks Road 97–99
St Mary Street 92
St Mary's Road 39
Terminus Station 89
University Road 123–124
Upper Deacon Road 114
Vosper Thornycroft 158
Western Docks 81, 82
Western Esplanade 62, 69, 71, 75–77
Westgate Street 80
Weston Lane 144–145
Winchester Road 131
Windsor Terrace 45–48, 51
Woodley Road 157
York Gate 15